**W9-BHR-321**

Math at the Bank

Place Value and Properties of Operations

Ian F. Mahaney

PowerKiDS press™

New York

Published in 2013 by The Rosen Publishing Group, Inc.
29 East 21st Street, New York, NY 10010

First Edition

Editor: Joanne Randolph
Book Design: Greg Tucker

Photo Credits: Cover, p. 16 © www.iStockphoto.com/YinYang; pp. 4–5 Comstock/Getty Images; pp. 7, 20–21 Ryan McVay/Photodisc/Getty Images; p. 8 AVAVA/Shutterstock.com; p. 9 Keith Brofsky/Photodisc/ Thinkstock; pp. 10–11 David McLain/Aurora/Getty Images; p. 12 Rocko and Betty/Workbook Stock/Getty Images; p. 13 R. Michael Ballard/Shutterstock.com; p. 14 Greg Tucker; p. 15 Flying Colours Ltd./Digital Vision/Thinkstock; p. 17 Marcel Jancovic/Shutterstock.com; p. 18 Glow Images/Getty Images; p. 19 BananaStock/Thinkstock.

Library of Congress Cataloging-in-Publication Data

Mahaney, Ian F.
  Math at the bank : place value and properties of operations / by Ian F. Mahaney. — 1st ed.
    p. cm. — (Core math skills)
Includes index.
ISBN 978-1-4488-9655-4 (library binding) — ISBN 978-1-4488-9768-1 (pbk.) —
ISBN 978-1-4488-9769-8 (6-pack)
1. Multiplication—Juvenile literature. 2. Addition—Juvenile literature. 3. Subtraction—Juvenile literature.
4. Place value (Mathematics)—Juvenile literature. 5. Banks and banking—Mathematics—Juvenile literature. I. Title.
QA115.M2274 2013
513.2'1—dc23
                                        2012024517

Manufactured in the United States of America

CPSIA Compliance Information: Batch #W13PK4: For Further Information contact Rosen Publishing, New York, New York at 1-800-237-9932

Contents

Math Is Everywhere

Sometimes when you are using math, it may not be obvious right away, such as when you are in the kitchen. At the bank, though, you can see the relationship to math right away.

Place value is an important concept at a bank. To count money, employees of the bank need to know which **digits** are the ones, tens, and hundreds.

The math operations addition, subtraction, multiplication, and division are important at banks, too. If a **bank teller** has five $20 bills, she can write a math sentence to find the total: 5 x $20 = $100. This book is about place value and the properties of operations used at a bank.

If a customer wants to take out $60, the teller can count out six $10 bills: 6 x $10 = $60. She could also count out three $20 bills: 3 x $20 = $60.

If a bank teller has six $100 bills, how much money does he have?

(See answers on p. 22)

Figure It Out

Ones, Tens, and More

By looking at the ones, tens, and hundreds digits, place value allows you to understand how large a number is. It also helps you compare two numbers to figure out which one is bigger.

You can use place value to compare 2,996 and 2,922. Each number has two thousands, so next compare the value of digits to the right of the thousands. Each number has nine hundreds, but the tens digit offers the solution. There are nine tens in 2,996 and two tens in 2,922. The greater number is 2,996, and that is expressed as 2,996 > 2,922. It helps to break down the digits to see the place value.

A chart like this one makes it easy to see the place values in a number.

Thousands	Hundreds	Tens	Ones
2	9	9	6
2	9	2	2

Our number system is based on the number 10. Every digit is 10 times greater than the digit to its right. The system is called base 10.

Is 3,582 or 3,528 larger? Make a chart like the on p. 6 to solve this.

(See answers on p. 22)

Figure It Out

Opening an Account

The first time many people use a bank is when they open an **account**. Often they will gather their money, count it, and decide how much they would like to **deposit** in the bank.

If you open a savings account with a $5 bill and a $20 bill, you deposit $5 + $20 = $25. Another way to

Has your teacher ever talked about turn-around facts? She is talking about the commutative property.

express this is with place value. It would look like this: $20 is two tens and $5 is five ones for a total of $20 + $5 = $25.

An important property of addition and multiplication is the **commutative property**. It says you can switch the order of two numbers you are adding or multiplying. The commutative property says that $5 + $20 = $20 + $5 = $25.

If you open a savings account with 5 $10 bills, how much do you have in the account? How much is in an account you open with 10 $5 bills?

(See answers on p. 22)

Figure It Out

More or Less?

Daniel and Kristen do chores for an **allowance**. Daniel saved $10 each week for 12 weeks. That is 12 x $10 = $120. Kristen saved $12 for 10 weeks. That is 10 x $12 = $120. Remember the commutative property says you are allowed to swap the numbers in a multiplication problem. Sorted for place value, 120 has one hundred, two tens, and zero ones:

Hundreds	Tens	Ones
1	2	0

Anne has saved $160 from babysitting.

Hundreds	Tens	Ones
1	6	0

To find out who of the three is going to deposit the most money, analyze the place value. All three have one hundred, but Anne has more tens. This means 160 > 120.

Bobby has $50 he earned from shoveling snow. If he adds that to $315 he has in his savings account, how much money does he have in the bank? What are the hundreds, tens, and ones values?

(See answers on p. 22)

Figure It Out

Make a Deposit

David has a paper route. He earns $47 in February, $50 in March, and $43 in April. Then he deposits the checks the newspaper company sent him.

David fills out a **deposit slip** at the bank, and he knows about an easy way to add the three amounts. The **associative property** of addition and multiplication

tells you that when adding or multiplying three or more numbers, you can do it in any order. For David, this means he can add $47 and $50 together and then add $43. He can also rearrange the numbers and add $47 and $43 first and add $50 to that: $47 + $43 + $50 = $90 + $50 = $140.

DEPOSIT TICKET

| V | CASH ▶ | *1000.00* |

DATE _____
DEPOSITS MAY NOT BE AVAILABLE FOR IMMEDIATE WITHDRAWAL

_____
SIGN HERE FOR CASH RECEIVED (IF REQUIRED) ★

(OR TOTAL FROM OTHER SIDE)

SUB TOTAL ▶ *1000.00*

★ LESS CASH RECEIVED ▶

$ *1000.00*

When you fill in a deposit slip, or ticket, you are using place value. The numbers to the right of the dot are cents. On the left side, the first box to the left of the dot is the ones place, the second box is the tens, and so on.

For three days, a bank is giving $7 to the first seven people who open savings accounts. How much will this cost the bank?

(See answers on p. 22)

Figure It Out

13

What to Do with Change?

You can split $1 into parts, or cents. The coins you may keep in a piggy bank can add up to dollars.

Have you seen money written as a **decimal**, like $2.14? The 2 is in the ones column. The period is the decimal point. It tells you that every digit to the right is part of a dollar. The 1 is in the tenths position and equals

You can use change to help you understand place value, too. Pennies stand for the ones. It takes 10 pennies to make a dime, the tens. It takes 100 pennies or 10 dimes to make a dollar.

one dime. The 4 is in the hundredths position and equals four pennies. Do you see that digits to the right of the decimal point follow place value rules, too? One dollar is 10 times greater than the digit to its right, the tenths digit.

If you have 21 nickels and eight quarters, what number will be in the ones place? What about the tens place? Add the money and write it down to help you see the answer: $3.05.

You have one dime. How many pennies does that equal?

(See answers on p. 22)

Figure It Out

Busy Bank Teller

A bank teller begins her day with $1,000 in cash. The first customer brings her a $200 check and $100 in cash. The teller now has $1,000 + $100 = $1,100 in cash. The second customer takes $100 cash out of his account. Taking money out of an account is called a **withdrawal**. The teller now has $1,100 − $100 = $1,000.

Bank tellers add and subtract all day long. They use place value to help themselves.

There is a machine at most banks called an ATM (automated teller machine). When you put your card in, you can deposit or withdraw cash from your account.

Did you notice what happened? The teller added $100 to her drawer and subtracted $100 from her drawer and ended with the same amount with which she began. This is because addition and subtraction are inverses. Inverses undo one another. Multiplication and division are also inverses.

You have $200 in your savings account and you deposit $50 one week and $25 the next week. You decide to withdraw $75 to buy presents for a friend. How much money do you have left in your account?

(See answers on p. 22)

Figure It Out

Money in the Vault

A bank's vault is where the bank keeps money. Vaults have thick walls to prevent theft or damage from fire. Many vaults have smaller vaults called safe-deposit boxes where customers can store **valuables**.

A vault is a big safe where banks keep money.

The **distributive property** of multiplication says that you can break up numbers by multiplying smaller numbers then adding the results together. Here is an example in the vault:

A man has 14 $100 bills. He can multiply $100 by 10 and 4 instead of multiplying $100 by 14 to figure out how much money he has. It would look like this:

14 x $100 =
(10 + 4) x $100 =
(10 x $100) + (4 x $100) =
$1,000 + $400 = $1,400.

In one day, customers withdraw 43 $10 bills from the ATM at a bank. How much money did the ATM dispense?

(See answers on p. 22)

Figure It Out

Math at the Bank

There is a lot of math to do at the bank. There are deposits to add and withdrawals to subtract. There is place value, tens, hundreds, or ones for every number seen in a bank. There is the inverse relationship between multiplication and division. Addition and subtraction are also inverses.

The relationship between operations goes further. A bank teller calculates the **balance** as the difference between a beginning balance and a withdrawal: $1,000 − $200 = $800. The ending balance plus the withdrawal equals the beginning balance: $800 + $200 = $1,000. This is called a fact family. See if you can find other relationships between numbers at a bank.

A customer begins a day with a $400 balance. He deposits $100 at 9 a.m. At noon, he withdraws $40 from the ATM. At 3 p.m., he needs more money and withdraws $60. What is his balance afterward?

(See answers on p. 22)

Figure It Out

Figure It Out: The Answers

Page 5: **The bank teller has 6 x $100 = $600.**

Page 7: **It helps to break down the digits to see the place value.**

Thousands	Hundreds	Tens	Ones
3	5	8	2
3	5	2	8

Since 3,582 has eight tens and 3,528 has two tens, 3,582 > 3,528.

Page 9: **The commutative property applies to multiplication. It says that 5 x $10 = 10 x $5 = $50. In both cases, you opened a savings account with $50.**

Page 11: **Bobby has $315 + $50 = $365 in the bank. There are three hundreds, six tens, and five ones in 365.**

Page 13: **To find out what it will cost the bank, multiply 3 by 7 by 7: 3 x 7 x $7 = 21 x $7 = $147.**

Page 15: **One dime means there is one in the tenths digit. One penny is in the hundredths digit. The tenths digit is 10 times greater than the hundredths digit so 1 dime = 10 pennies.**

Page 17: **You have $200. You start with $200 and then add $50 and $25. $200 + ($50 + $25) = $200 + $75 = $275. If you then decide to spend $75, you are back to where you started: $275 - $75 = $200 in your account.**

Page 19: **Using the distributive property for multiplication, the ATM dispensed 43 x $10 = (40 + 3) x $10 = (40 x $10) + (3 x $10) = $400 + $30 = $430.**

Page 21: **His balance after the deposit is $400 + $100 = $500. After he visits the ATM at noon, his balance is $500 – $40 = $460. After the second withdrawal, his balance is $460 – $60 = $400.**

Glossary

account (uh-KOWNT) The place where a bank keeps money set aside for a person.

allowance (uh-LOW-ents) Money given to children, sometimes as a trade for chores.

associative property (uh-SOH-shee-ay-tiv PRO-pur-tee) A rule in addition and multiplication that says that when three or more numbers are added or multiplied together, any two can be added or multiplied first and still find the same result.

balance (BAL-ens) The amount of money in a bank account.

bank teller (BANGKTEH-ler) An employee of a bank who helps customers with their accounts.

commutative property (kuh-MYOO-tuh-tiv PRO-pur-tee) A rule in multiplication that says the order in which numbers are multiplied does not change the result.

decimal (DEH-suh-mul) A part of 100.

deposit (dih-PAH-zut) To put money into the bank.

deposit slip (dih-PAH-zut SLIP) A piece of paper the bank uses to record money deposited.

digits (DIH-jits) Positions of single numbers. Tens and ones are digits.

distributive property (dih-STRIB-yoo-tiv PRO-pur-tee) A rule in multiplication that allows bigger numbers to be split into smaller numbers.

place value (PLAYS VAL-yoo) The ones, tens, and hundreds of a number.

valuables (VAL-yoo-uh-bulz) Things important to a person or things worth a lot of money.

withdrawal (with-DRAW-ul) Taking money out of the bank.

Index

Websites

Due to the changing nature of Internet links, PowerKids Press has developed an online list of websites related to the subject of this book. This site is updated regularly. Please use this link to access the list: www.powerkidslinks.com/cms/bank/